Additional Praise for *Guerrillas of Grace*

"Loder's prayers are subversive and liberating, revealing and inspiring, sneaky and seductive—just like God is. Loder is above all a poet, an artist, testing, playing with, creating words and rhythms that can carry us beyond the edge, beyond the familiar into a new place where revelations abound and renewal is possible. Through Loder's hungry, restless search for God, we gain courage to stumble alongside in our own halting, hopeful prayers."
—Dr. Caryn McTighe Musil, vice president of the Office of Diversity, Equity, and Global Initiatives, Association of American College and Universities

"It is the tickle of Loder's inspirations spread before us on the attractive pages of *Guerrillas of Grace* that cause us to giggle and than perhaps to gag and, catching our breath, to grope for the grace of God that is always available but usually underutilized."
—*The United Methodist Reporter* (Dr. John G. McElhenney)

"This collection offers the reader a plethora of images that tumble effortlessly forth to feed hungry souls on dark nights. Here is a minister-writer who is unafraid of crying out his complaints, confessions, denials, and dreams—all the while not taking himself too seriously. Thanks be!"
—Rev. Joan E. Hemenway, board-certified chaplain and clinical pastoral education supervisor in the Yale-New Haven System

"[This is] not a book for those who already have answers. It speaks to everyone who is struggling with the hard questions of life. Loder's prayers are born out of passion, hard work, and openness. In all, it is a beautifully written celebration of life that dares to sing of God's surprising grace in the midst of an often torn and painful world. Anyone who yearns for hope that is real, because it has been experienced, will find this book of prayers to be for them."
—Rev. Margie J. Mayson, pastor of Outreach and Discipleship, Asbury First United Methodist Church, Rochester, New York

Additional Praise for Ted Loder's Prayers

"There's more grace in Loder's poems than in all the sweet talk about Jesus in America."
—*Circuit Rider*

"Ted Loder's prayers are written in the familiar cadence of everyday language, but leavened with echoes of the inspired awe, wonder and praise of the ancient scriptures."
—Dr. Bob Edgar, general secretary, National Council of the Churches of Christ in the USA and former congressman from Pennsylvania

"Ted Loder is the poet of prayer. I know no one who so movingly and honestly brings us before God in prayers that touch the personal and the social dimensions of our lives."
—Tex Sample, coordinator of The Network for the Study of U.S. Lifestyles, Rogers professor emeritus of Church and Society, Saint Paul School of Theology

"Does prayer have to be stilted or sentimental? Can it express real feeling without getting weepy? Ted Loder shows how prayer can escape these pitfalls and become authentic."
—Harvey Cox, Hollis professor of Divinity, Harvard University; author of *Common Prayers*

"Loder's prayers are a lantern to illumine the wonders, terrors, and miracles of our passing days."
—Rev. William Sloane Coffin, pastor emeritus, Riverside Church, New York; most recently, author of *Credo*

"Loder is a creative and prophetic poet who will not stay in the pulpit."
—W. Paul Jones, M.Div., PhD., former professor at Yale University, Princeton University, and Saint Paul School of Theology; author of *A Season in the Desert*

"So refreshingly unpretentious and honest . . . Loder is a man who lives both within and beyond the lines of his religious tradition and the norms of our culture. [He] is a social activist with the soul of a mystic who understands the longings of ordinary people and the profoundness of the gospel."
—John W. Vannorsdall, former chaplain, Yale University; president emeritus, Lutheran Seminary, Philadelphia

Guerrillas of Grace

OTHER BOOKS BY TED LODER:

The Haunt of Grace: Responses to the Mystery of God's Presence

My Heart in My Mouth: Prayers for Our Lives

Tracks in the Straw: Tales Spun from the Manger

Wrestling the Light: Ache and Awe in the Human/Divine Struggle

20th Anniversary Edition

GUERRILLAS *of* Grace

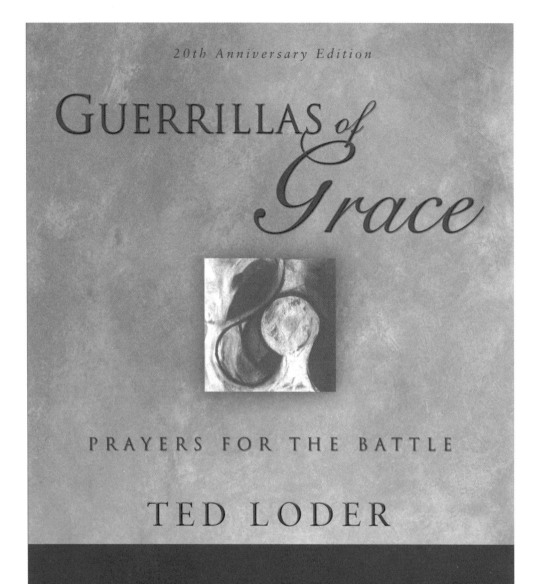

PRAYERS FOR THE BATTLE

TED LODER

Augsburg Books
MINNEAPOLIS

GUERRILLAS OF GRACE
Prayers for the Battle

Copyright © 1981 Ted Loder, International Copyright Secured.
All Rights Reserved. Except for brief quotations
in critical articles or reviews, no part of this book may be reproduced in any manner
without prior written permission from the publisher. Write to: Permissions,
Augsburg Fortress, Box 1209, Minneapolis, MN 55440.

Large-quantity purchases or custom editions of this book are available
at a discount from the publisher. For more information,
contact the sales department at Augsburg Fortress, Publishers,
800-328-4648, or write to: Sales Director, Augsburg Fortress, Publishers,
P. O. Box 1209, Minneapolis, MN 55440-1209.

Library of Congress Cataloging-in-Publication Data
Loder, Ted, 1930-
Guerrillas of grace / by Ted Loder.—20th anniversary ed.
p. cm.
Includes index.
ISBN 0-8066-9054-2
1. Prayers. I. Title.
BV245.L57 2005
242'.8—dc22   2004022616

Cover design by Laurie Ingram
Book design by Michelle L. N. Cook
Drawings by Ed Kerns

The paper used in this publication meets the minimum requirements
of American National Standard for Information Sciences—
Permanence of Paper for Printed Library Materials, ANSI Z329.48-1984. ⊖ ™

Manufactured in the U.S.A.

for Jan . . .
guerrilla of grace,
companion in faith,
gift of joy.

Contents

Ground Me in Your Grace

Eternal One,
    Silence
        from whom my words come;
    Questioner
        from whom my questions arise;
    Lover
        of whom all my loves are hints;
    Disturber
        in whom alone I find my rest;
    Mystery
        in whose depths I find healing
            and myself;
enfold me now in your presence;
    restore to me your peace;
        renew me through your power;
            and ground me in your grace.

Probing . . .

Why would anyone call a book of prayers, *Guerrillas of Grace*? The two images, "guerrillas" and "grace," seem to be an unlikely, if not contradictory, conjunction. And yet . . . are they really?

Somewhere I read a description of poets as "guerrillas of beauty." I suppose it is fitting that I can't find the article, or even identify it, but the phrase struck me and took captive a piece of my imagination, as if demonstrating the power of the image. Or maybe it would be more accurate to say the phrase *liberated* a piece of my imagination. I began to see "guerrillas of beauty" as applying to the risky and exciting struggles of people attempting to live out their faith in more free and joyful ways in the midst of difficult, resistant, often even oppressive circumstances. I began to understand the phrase as applying well to people who pray and to the prayers they utter.

Yet, as important as I believe beauty is, and as powerful as I have experienced it to be, I think it is even more provocative to call those who pray, and the prayers themselves, "guerrillas of grace."

The notion of guerrillas seems to be rooted in the ancient Judeo-Christian tradition. The Old Testament prophets can easily be conceived of as guerrillas doing battle with the established powers of their day; and their thundering, poetic words and images surely can be read as forms of prayer. Certainly Jesus was the pre-eminent guerrilla of grace; he confronted repressive institutions and liberated captive minds and hearts with his words and his life. A prime weapon in his effort was prayer, and it is little wonder that he taught his disciples to pray.

The early Christians understood and rallied to Paul's battle cry: "For we are not contending against flesh and blood, but against principalities, against powers, against the world rulers of this present darkness . . ." They, along with Christians across the ages, confirmed the idea that we are guerrillas.

There are two or three characteristics of guerrillas that give particular relevance to the use of that image to describe Christians. By any of our usual measures, guerrillas are a weaker force set against a superior and more organized power, a power which exerts both subtle and blatant pressures to conform. Such pressures are not commonly or quickly perceived or interpreted as oppressive, but frequently something in them is experienced as, at least, vaguely stifling to the spirit.

Guerrillas, then, are engaged in the battle to reclaim some territory, or some part of life, for a higher purpose, a truer cause. To wed guerrilla with grace suggests that the truer cause is God's kingdom. Since the "principalities and powers" are never completely "out there," but also stomp and rumble "within," a significant piece of the life to be reclaimed or liberated is the prayer himself or herself. In an unavoidable way the struggle begins—and begins again and again and again—with choosing sides. Choose one side and you're a conformist; choose another and you're a guerrilla!

Doesn't "guerrilla" describe the contemporary church in many third world countries? Christians in those countries have been cut off from typical religious support systems, yet have survived and grown in obviously hostile environments. Wasn't Dr. Martin Luther King Jr.'s civil rights movement in the 1960s a nonviolent guerrilla force, born and nurtured in the black church? Don't you suppose prayer was a critical part of what those Christians were about?

It is also important to note that guerrillas usually work in groups. In some fashion we never pray alone. We always pray toward someone and with someone—namely, whoever resides within us as teacher, friend, enemy, burden, brother, sister, spirit. However private our prayers may seem, we are still the cloud of witnesses when we pray (just as we are when we think or act). So the prayers in this volume, though framed in personal terms, could easily be used as corporate prayers, and in many instances have been. The point is that both grace and guerrilla are relational terms.

And finally, guerrillas are never quite so desperate as they are confident. They believe they are fighting on the winning side, in spite of any and all appearances to the contrary. We have to be exceedingly careful in even considering this characteristic, for abuses perpetrated by religious arrogance are all too evident and painful. Still, guerrillas are willing to give their lives, if necessary, because they believe the cause for which they struggle, and which struggles in them, will finally prevail. Even so, the pray-er is always saying, one way or another, ". . . thy kingdom come."

Yet, prayer is always against the odds set by logic, by scientism, by realism. So, it is always against the odds of our own skepticism and doubt. Even when prayer is inchoate in something that sounds like a curse or a moan or a desperate plea or a spontaneous "whoopee," there is a gut deep, intuitive refusal to accept the odds or to calculate too closely either the limits of the possible or the sneakiness of grace.

When the prayer is more intentional, the guerrilla raid may at least suspend those odds for a bit longer and open the one who prays to broader dimensions of reality than we have entertained before. Once that happens, there can never again be quite an end of it. Some part of us is taken captive or set free, and that shift changes the world a little. At those moments we also (and rightly) refuse to calculate what might be changed in the world beyond us, what might be gracefully released in it by our prayers.

It may be presumptuous to call oneself, and one's prayers, "guerrillas of grace." Grace is the sole property of God. It distinguishes the quality of God's love from human love. But then, how does grace become operative in the world? What is the process? Admittedly, those are large and complicated questions about which volumes have been and will be written, and which are beyond the scope of this introduction.

Still, one simple answer, and wondrous, is that God's grace operates in the world quite independently of us. Prayer is one way of attempting to focus on grace, to pay attention to it, to praise it. The French mystic Simone Weil is right in saying, "Perfect attention is prayer." Surely it is true that any attempts to be attentive, however imperfect, are also prayers. Imagination is crucial to paying attention, for attention is far more than observation. Imagination involves penetrating something, or being open to being penetrated by something, in order to sense its meaning, its possibilities, its depths, its "story."

Another simple answer, and equally wondrous, is that praying itself is part of the process by which grace becomes operative in the world. The pray-er becomes a participating point of the entry and expansion of grace, so that Augustine is also right in saying, "Without God, we cannot; without us, God will not."

In this sense imagination is crucial as a way of pre-figuring the shape or course the future may take. Imagination is an indispensable faculty in the process of deciding and acting toward the future. Thus, prayer can be playful because the imagination plays with possibilities, putting them together in different combinations before we begin to enact them. Since children are naturally adept at such play, perhaps that is one reason Jesus said, "Unless you turn and become as children, you will never enter the kingdom of heaven." Since pre-figuring is an ongoing process, the imagination is always engaged in adjusting and reformulating. Thus, the future is always being partly created by the imagination of the pray-er and the prayer.

Therefore, since paying attention is one condition of prayer, the occasion of attending is a guerrilla action through which grace takes, or liberates, new ground in the praying person. Yet, through the mysterious dynamics of exchange, prayers and pray-ers themselves are the guerrilla action by which grace helps shape the future: ". . . without us, God will not." Prayer, through the process of imagination, becomes part of the answer to the remainder of the question, "Without us, God will not do *what*?" Prayer, as is faith or hope or love, is always guerrilla action in the world of time on behalf of the eternal.

Personally, my prayers happen in two ways. The first way, I believe, is nearly universal: the urgent, spontaneous outbursts, if not of half-formed words, fragmented and fleeting, then surely of a surge of emotions, sensations of awe or wonder or yearning which suddenly flood in and overflow to connect me, perhaps only in dim awareness, to the springs and rhythms of life and its impenetrable mysteries. I suppose only mystics and poets could, or should, even attempt to communicate these kinds of prayers with others, though these prayers are perhaps the most common. They are intensely personal and the type I most frequently mutter or moan.

The second way my prayers happen is as the more articulated works of my imagination. These are the kind of prayers contained in this book. Imagination is a basic faculty of faith and poetry, indeed, of any creative act. Imagination is surely one quality of God's image in us, just as is the capacity to love. For me, imagination is a way of gathering up the present and the immediate past—the things, persons, experiences to which I have been attentive, or sometimes just dully present—and putting them into images, into language which I hurl toward God and toward the future. Prayer is one way I participate in the ongoing creation. Prayer, through imagination, opens me and (I am presumptuous enough to contend) opens the future to new options, different possibilities. Imagination is a way of re-interpreting the past, re-viewing the present, and previewing the future and the way I can act toward it. Imagination is a way of interrupting the programs for repetition into which I so easily set myself.

I have heard, with only partial understanding but with imagination, that the images of artists and poets often precede and instruct scientific discovery. If that is in any way true, the implications boggle the mind. Could it be that the images of poets and artists (and pray-ers)

not only precede scientific discovery in some instances, but that they actually help *create* what the scientist later discovers? Indeed, could prayer be one of the fundamental ways "the universe becomes conscious of itself," to use that intriguing phrase by which some cosmologists explain not only how the universe seems to be unfolding, but why it is unfolding at all? But enough! I have strayed into depths well over my head.

Still, the depths themselves are an essential condition to acknowledge in prayer, at least for me. Depths swirl about the word "mystery," affirming that when we have to do with God, deep mystery is always one of the first conditions that pertain. God always outdistances our thoughts, words, knowledge, creeds, litanies, lives; outdistances them either because God is too simple for us to apprehend, or too complex for us to comprehend, or both.

An illustrative instance of what I am suggesting is the effort to de-sexualize the language and thinking of the church and to apply traditionally "feminine" characteristics to God. Such an effort is accurate and overdue! It opens us to dimensions of God we have missed and opens to God ways of being with us that have been denied. This experience of opening demonstrates what the richness of the depths of mystery means when referred to God, and how attentively exploring those depths liberates more territory for grace. That we explore those depths, and they us, makes us guerrillas of grace. But the unfathomable quality of mystery reminds us that it is the grace of God that we are exploring.

Mystery means that, in spite of all our efforts, all our insights, discoveries, and experiences, we will never do much more than touch the hem of God's robe. It is enough that such touching brings healing. It is too much, idolatrously too much, to claim more than a very little information about the wearer of the robe. And even that little information, we can claim only with enormous humility. However, humility is the twin of trust.

It has been said, referring to the temptation to which biblical literalists often succumb, that we should never confuse the love letter with the lover. We all have our version of such literalism, our dogmaticisms, our exaggerated (if unadmitted) claims of knowledge. Humble acknowledgement of mystery delivers us from the imprisonment of such certainties into the awesome dimensions of possibilities. Trust begins there. So, in some primitive way, does prayer.

Historically, the church has used the term "holy" to refer to what I mean by the word "mystery." My bias for the word mystery is grounded in the awareness that holiness is a term which often has been too well defined and too aggressively applied in too many inquisitions. Jesus gave the mystery a personal name, as did the prophets, but Jesus did not thereby eliminate or domesticate the mystery. The point is, mystery simply reminds us that God is free to be God in ways we have no knowledge of at all.

Since God is free to respond to prayers in surprising, sneaky ways (you may have noticed I like the word "sneaky") that no one can prescribe, we also are free to do new things, pray new ways, imagine new images, find different words. We are never required to be liturgical literalists. We are never restricted merely to repeating the prayers of our tradition, however beautiful and helpful. Nor are there "right" prayers, or "right" ways of praying, or "right" words with which to pray. Guerrillas *extend* grace, not encapsulate it.

So, the second way I pray, articulating from my imagination, involves work! There are people who insist that the only prayers which are valid are those offered spontaneously at the immediate inspiration of the Holy Spirit. Such prayers certainly are valid, but they are also usually more inchoate than inspired or inspiring, and they tend to be repetitious and dull. I believe the Holy Spirit inspires me just as well when I am struggling to think, to attend, to write, to find the appropriate words, symbols, images which will open me, and perhaps those who pray with me, to those new perceptions and possibilities that hint of grace.

Poet John Ciardi states that the poets' morality resides in "never cheapening their choices" of words or images. I concur and think it is almost immoral for a person consistently to cheapen his or her prayer choices by trying to avoid the cost of paying attention, for attention does have a cost. I think it is almost immoral, and certainly lazy, for anyone not to work carefully and honestly to shape prayers since, ". . . without us, God will not." And probably "God will not" without our best efforts! Who dares to be a sloppy guerrilla? Who deserves one?

So, my attempts to pray, to use my imagination as I pray, involve three factors. The first is to express—through words, images, symbols—what I see, feel, attend to and experience, but to do so in ways that both sharpen my awareness and perhaps provide me and my companion guerrillas a shift in perception, a slightly different way of seeing, interpreting, and responding to life. In that shift, however slight, I believe my prayers are already being answered. The guerrilla process has begun because the shift involves probing, reaching, playing with different images and options which are changing me. Grace is sneaky!

The second aspect of imaginative praying is to be open to words, thoughts, feelings, visions, and alternatives which bubble up or float down when I am struggling to find a way to be honest and creative and to have some integrity in that prayer process. Sometimes the muse does ride, or better, the Spirit does move. But often the impulse or image that comes seems, at first blush, to be too radical or profane or outrageous to be acceptable or to use. But that may be exactly the time to work at staying open and following the lead, the intuition, the inspiration. Passion, which is surely part of praying just

as centering and quietness are, is not always nice or proper! Unfortunately, passion seldom seems to be part of what we have been taught is involved in being religious or praying. Passion touches on one reason I like the prayer included in this volume which adds to the familiar phrase describing God as being the one "from whom no secrets are hid" another phrase: "and none need to be."* Grace is sneaky, not superficial.

The third factor in my praying is to let my prayer carry me. I saw an expression somewhere which asked, "If you aren't carried away, why go?" There is at least some delightful truth in that, except that the rest also needs saying: namely, for the most part, you don't get carried away if you don't hoist your sails to the wind by doing the work of preparation and persistence.

But often, because of our anxieties about control and losing it, when the wind starts to blow we tend to lower our sails. Once new possibilities start to emerge, once the future gets imaged differently, once the impulse tugs to try an option other than the familiar rut, then the inner and outer argument begins. The limits of what is possible start to get calculated "realistically" again. The ballast of odds becomes heavy. The territory which had begun to be freed by the guerrillas of grace gets retaken by the armies of conformity and caution. Is this true for you, too, or do I refer only to myself?

It has taken me a long time and hard struggle even to begin to wrestle effectively

*"I Am So Thankful to Be Alive," page 46

with this third factor. Mostly it still pins me without giving me a blessing. I've discovered that it has something to do with expectations. On the one hand, we can expect too much, too fast, and give up praying when it doesn't happen. Jesus, and saints since, have said much about this danger. Yet, on the other hand, we can get frightened and give up praying when different options do emerge and we are nudged toward them. However much we talk about our longing for change in ourselves and the world, the actual prospect of that change, and the cost of it in terms of engaging in battle with the powers of conformity, produces some ambivalence at best. Ambivalence generates resistance. It is hard to get carried away when we're hanging on tightly to the familiar.

I'm discovering that getting carried away doesn't necessarily mean moving at the speed of light or to the gates of heaven (or whatever you envision as a quick escape, or a safe haven from the toil and trouble of change). It may mean being carried away as a stoker on a slow freighter, as it were. For me, the process of being carried away does happen slowly, even painfully, albeit joyfully, an inch a day, another at night, for a lifetime. But I am getting there. Grace is sneaky and persistent!

Being carried away also involves, for me, some intentional participation in the mystery, some attempt to embody the images and exhibit the perceptions of some piece of my prayers. It involves willingly, perhaps foolishly, taking the risk about which we are warned in the old joke, "Be careful what you pray for; you may get it." But, isn't that possibility precisely why pray-ers are guerrillas of grace?

So you see, I cannot believe that praying doesn't make a difference. If it doesn't, what else could?

For at last I believe life itself is a prayer,
    and the prayers we say shape the lives we live,
just as the lives we live shape the prayers we say;
    and it all shapes the kingdom which expresses itself in and among us,
        and for which we are guerrillas.
I hope these prayers help you to take some new territory,
    to liberate imaginatively some part of your life,
        my sister and brother guerrillas.
        ". . . thy kingdom come . . ."

—Ted Loder

Prayers
OF QUIETNESS
& LISTENING

Listen to Me Under My Words

O God,
I come to you now
as a child to my Mother,
    out of the cold which numbs
        into the warm who cares.
Listen to me inside,
    under my words
        where the shivering is,
    in the fears
        which freeze my living,
    in the angers
        which chafe my attending,
    in the doubts
        which chill my hoping,
    in the events
        which shrivel my thanking,
    in the pretenses
        which stiffen my loving.

Listen to me, Lord,
as a Mother,
    and hold me warm,
        and forgive me.
Soften my experiences
    into wisdom,
my pride
    into acceptance,
my longing
    into trust,
and soften me
    into love
        and to others
          and to you.

Guide Me into an Unclenched Moment

Gentle me,
Holy One,
into an unclenched moment,
    a deep breath,
        a letting go
            of heavy expectancies,
                of shriveling anxieties,
                    of dead certainties,
that, softened by the silence,
    surrounded by the light,
        and open to the mystery,
I may be found by wholeness,
    upheld by the unfathomable,
        entranced by the simple,
            and filled with the joy
                that is you.

Hear Me Quickly, Lord

Hear me quickly, Lord,
for my mind soon wanders to other things
    I am more familiar with
        and more concerned about
            than I am with you.
O Timeless God, for whom I do not have time,
catch me with a sudden stab of beauty
    or pain
        or regret
that will catch me up short for a moment
to look hard enough at myself—
    the unutterable terror
        and hope within me
and, so, to be caught by you.

Words will not do, Lord.
Listen to my tears,
    for I have lost much
        and fear more.
Listen to my sweat,
    for I wake at night
        overwhelmed by darkness and strange dreams.
Listen to my sighs,
    for my longing surges like the sea—
        urgent, mysterious and beckoning.
Listen to my heart beat,
    for I want to live fully
        and stay death forever.
Listen to my breathing,
    for I gulp after something like holiness.
Listen to my clenched teeth,
    for I gnaw at my grudges
        and forgive myself as reluctantly
           as I forgive others.

Listen to my growling gut,
    for I hunger for bread and intimacy.
Listen to my curses,
    for I am angry at the way the world
        comes down on me sometimes,
            and I sometimes on it.
Listen to my cracking knuckles,
    for I hold very tightly to myself
        and anxiously squeeze myself into other's expectations,
            and them into mine,
     and then shake my fists at you
        for disappointing me.
Listen to my sex,
    for I seek fulfillment
        through the man-woman differences
            and beyond the differences,
                a new, common humanity.
Listen to my foot falls,
    for I stumble to bring good tidings to someone.
Listen to my groans,
    for I ache toward healing.
Listen to my worried weariness,
    for my work matters much to me
        and needs help.
Listen to my tension,
    for I stretch toward accepting who I am
        and who I cannot be.
Listen to my wrinkles,
    for growing years make each day
        singularly precious to me
            and bring eternity breathtakingly close.

Listen to my hunched back,
    for sometimes I can't bear
        the needs and demands of the world anymore
           and want to put it down,
              give it back to you.
Listen to my laughter,
    for there are friends and mercy
        and the day grows longer,
           and something urges me to thank.
Listen to my humming,
    for sometimes I catch all unaware
        the rhythms of creation
and then music without words
        rises in me to meet it,
           and there is the joy of romping children
              and dancing angels.
Listen to my blinking eyes,
    for at certain moments
        when sunlight strikes just right,
        or stars pierce the darkness just enough,
        or clouds roll around just so,
        or snow kisses the earth into quietness,
    everything is suddenly transparent,
        and crows announce the presence of another world,
        and dogs bark at it,
and something in me is pure enough
        for an instant
to see your kingdom in a glance,
and so to praise you in a gasp—
    quick,
        then gone,
           but it is enough.
Listen to me quickly, Lord.

Calm Me into a Quietness

Now,
O Lord,
calm me into a quietness
    that heals
        and listens,
and molds my longings
    and passions,
        my wounds
            and wonderings
into a more holy
    and human
        shape.

I Need to Breathe Deeply

Eternal Friend,
grant me an ease
to breathe deeply of this moment,
    this light,
        this miracle of now.
Beneath the din and fury
    of great movements
        and harsh news
            and urgent crises,
make me attentive still
    to good news,
        to small occasions,
            and the grace of what is possible
                for me to be,
                to do,
                  to give,
                    to receive,
that I may miss neither my neighbor's gift
    nor my enemy's need.

Precious Lord,
grant me
    a sense of humor
        that adds perspective to compassion,
    gratitude
        that adds persistence to courage,
    quietness of spirit
        that adds irrepressibility to hope,
    openness of mind
        that adds surprise to joy;
that with gladness of heart
I may link arm and aim
with the One who saw signs of your kingdom
    in salt and yeast,
        pearls and seeds,
            travelers and tax collectors,
            sowers and harlots,
                foreigners and fishermen,
and who opens my eyes with these signs
    and my ears with the summons
        to follow to something more
            of justice and joy.

In the Silence, Name Me

Holy One,
    untamed
        by the names
           I give you,
in the silence
    name me,
that I may know
    who I am,
hear the truth
    you have put into me,
trust the love
    you have for me,
        which you call me to live out
           with my sisters and brothers
             in your human family.

Help Me Listen

O Holy One,
I hear and say so many words,
yet yours is the word I need.
Speak now,
and help me listen;
and, if what I hear is silence,
    let it quiet me,
        let it disturb me,
            let it touch my need,
                let it break my pride,
                    let it shrink my certainties,
                        let it enlarge my wonder.

O Eternal One, it would be easier for me to pray
    if I were clear
        and of a single mind and a pure heart;
    if I could be done hiding from myself
        and from you, even in my prayers.
But, I am who I am,
    mixture of motives and excuses,
        blur of memories,
            quiver of hopes,
    knot of fear,
        tangle of confusion,
            and restless with love, for love.
I wander somewhere between
    gratitude and grievance,
        wonder and routine,
            high resolve and undone dreams,
                generous impulses and unpaid bills.
Come, find me, Lord.
Be with me exactly as I am.
Help me find me, Lord.
    Help me accept what I am,
        so I can begin to be yours.
Make of me something small enough to snuggle,
    young enough to question,
        simple enough to giggle,
            old enough to forget,
                foolish enough to act for peace;
    skeptical enough to doubt
        the sufficiency of anything but you,
    and attentive enough to listen
        as you call me out of the tomb of my timidity
            into the chancy glory of my possibilities
            and the power of your presence.

Grant Me an Enchantment of Heart

O God of children and clowns,
    as well as martyrs and bishops,
somehow you always seem to tumble
    a jester or two of light
        through the cracks of my proud defense
           into the shadows of my sober piety.
Grant me, now, an enchantment of heart
    that, for a moment, the calliope of your kingdom
        may entice my spirit, laughing,
           out of my sulky self-preoccupations
        into a childlike delight
           in the sounds and silences
              that hum of grace;
so I may learn again
that life is never quite as serious as I suppose,
yet more precious than I dare take for granted,
    even for a moment;
that I may be released
    into the possibilities of the immediate,
and rush,
    smudge souled as I am,
        to join the parade of undamned fools
           who see the ridiculous in the sublime,
           the sublime in the ridiculous;
and so dare to take pratfalls for love,
    walk tightropes for justice,
        tame lions for peace,
and rejoice to travel light,
    knowing there is little I have or need
        except my brothers and sisters to love,
           you to trust,
              and your stars to follow home.

Eternal God,
lead me now
    out of the familiar setting
       of my doubts and fears,
    beyond my pride
       and my need to be secure
into a strange and graceful ease
    with my true proportions
       and with yours;
that in boundless silence
    I may grow
       strong enough to endure
          and flexible enough to share
            your grace.

Give Me Ears to Hear

Lord,
I believe
    my life is touched by you,
        that you want something for me,
           and of me.
Give me ears
    to hear you,
eyes
    to see the tracing of your finger,
and a heart
    quickened by the motions
        of your Spirit.

Prayers
OF THANKS
& PRAISE

Praise from All Creatures

Praise be to you, O Lord,
who spins shining stars across the wondrous heavens
    and stretches out the seas,
who lifts the dawn into place
    and sets boundaries for night,
who awes the earth with storms
    and gentles it with green,
who gives everything a season
    and breathes life and love into the dust of me.
Praise be to you.

Praise in all things,
    for all things:
the soft slant of sunlight,
    the sweat of battle,
a song in the wilderness,
    the evening breeze,
the deep breath,
    the tended wound,
mercy, quietness, a friend;
for the miracles of the daily,
    the mysteries of the eternal.
Praise be to you.

Praise from all creatures,
    laughers and list-makers,
        wonders and worriers,
            poets and plodders and prophets,
                the wrinkled, the newborn,
                    the whale, and the worm,
                        from all, and from me.
Praise, praise be to you
for amazing grace.

Bless What Eludes My Grasp

Lord, so many things skitter through my mind,
and I give chase to gather them
   and hold them up in a bunch to you,
but they go this way and that
   while I go that way and this . . .
So, gather me up instead
and bless what eludes my grasp but not yours:
   trees and bees, fireflies and butterflies,
   roses and barbecues, and people . . .
Lord, the people . . . bless the people:
   birthday people,
      giving birth people,
         being born people;
   conformed people,
      dying people,
         dead people;
   hostaged people,
      banged up people,
         held down people;
   leader people,
      lonely people,
         limping people;
   hungry people,
      surfeited people,
         indifferent people;
   first world people,
      second world people,
         third world people;
   one world people,
      your people,
         all people.
Bless them, Lord.
Bless what eludes my grasp but not yours.

Praise Be to You for Life

Praise be to you, O Lord, for life
    and for my intense desire to live;
praise be to you for the mystery of love
    and for my intense desire to be a lover;
praise be to you for this day
    and another chance to live and love.

Thank you, Lord,
    for friends who stake their claim in my heart,
    for enemies who disturb my soul and bump my ego,
    for tuba players,
        and story tellers,
            and trapeze troupes.
Thank you, Lord,
    for singers of songs,
    for teachers of songs,
        who help me sing along the way,
    . . . and for listeners.
Thank you, Lord,
    for those who attempt beauty
        rather than curse ugliness,
    for those who take stands
        rather than take polls,
    for those who risk being right
        rather than pandering to be liked,
    for those who do something
        rather than talking about everything.

Lord, grant me grace, then,
and a portion of your spirit
that I may so live
    as to give others cause
        to be thankful for me,
thankful because I have not forgotten
    how to hope,
        how to laugh,
           how to say, "I'm sorry,"
    how to forgive,
        how to bind up wounds,
           how to dream,
    how to cry,
        how to pray,
    how to love when it is hard,
        and how to dare when it is dangerous.
Undamn me, Lord,
that praise may flow more easily from me
    than wants,
thanks more readily
    than complaints.
Praise be to you, Lord, for life;
praise be to you for another chance to live.

I Praise You for What Is Yet to Be

Wondrous Worker of Wonders,
I praise you, not alone for what has been,
    or for what is,
        but for what is yet to be,
for you are gracious beyond all telling of it.

I praise you
that out of the turbulence of my life
    a kingdom is coming,
        is being shaped even now
            out of my slivers of loving,
                my bits of trusting,
                my sprigs of hoping,
                my tootles of laughing,
                my drips of crying,
                my smidgens of worshiping;
that out of my songs and struggles,
    out of my griefs and triumphs,
        I am gathered up and saved,
for you are gracious beyond all telling of it.

I praise you
that you turn me loose
    to go with you to the edge of now and maybe,
        to welcome the new,
            to see my possibilities,
                to accept my limits,
and yet begin living to the limit
    of passion and compassion
        until, released by joy,
            I uncurl to other people
                and to your kingdom coming,
for you are gracious beyond all telling of it.

Thank You for Each Moment

Lord, thank you for each moment,
    for the blue-sky moment,
        the softening earth, the freshening wind,
    for the sap flowing,
        the bird nesting, the yellow bush,
    for my full heart
        and the joy rising in me.
Soften me
    to receive whatever comes as a gift
        and to praise you in it.

Lord, thank you for each moment,
    for the twilight moment,
        the pause, the good tired,
    for the quiet reflection,
        the slowing down, the mysterious sunset,
    for my contented heart
        and the wisdom growing inside me.
Gentle me
    to feel whatever comes as a gift
        and to praise you in it.

Lord, thank you for each moment,
    for the midnight moment,
        the loneliness, the fretful wondering,
    for the watchful stars,
        the long ache, the sleepless wait,
for my restless heart
    and the hope straining in me.
Focus me
    to see whatever comes as a gift
        and to praise you in it.

Lord, thank you for each moment,
    for the high-noon moment,
        the job, the necessary routine,
    for the sweaty struggle,
        the high-risk challenge, the impulse to change,
    for my fierce heart
        and the courage gathering in me.
Ground me
    to wrestle with whatever comes as a gift
        and to praise you in it.

Lord, thank you for each moment,
    for the shared moment,
        the listening, the unguarded word,
    for the fragile openness,
        the ready smile, the accepted difference,
    for my passionate heart
        and the trust rooting in me.
Stretch me
    to grow with whatever comes as a gift
        and to praise you in it.

Lord, thank you for each moment,
    for the charged moment,
        the confrontation, the accurate demand,
    for the hard decision,
        the breathless gamble, the unexpected growing,
    for my intense heart
        and the truth expanding in me.
Excite me
    to be open to whatever comes as a gift
        and to praise you in it.

Lord, thank you for each moment,
    for the holy moment,
        the music, the child's eyes,
    for the sunlight,
        the touch, the tears,
    for the trembling pleasure,
        the unutterable beauty, the breathing,
    for the life and love and heart in me, aware,
        and the wholeness spreading in me.
Touch me
    through whatever comes as a gift
        that I may be graceful
           and praise you in it all.

Persistent Friend, Insistent Enemy,
  from whom no secret is hid (and none need to be),
    out of the thoughts and feelings which whirl within,
      I grope for language to carry to you my secrets
        and all the wonders that seize my heart.
Praise be to you
  for holding me in the womb of mystery
    through all the eons of creation until now
  and raising me to life
    in this time and place.

I am so thankful to be alive—
  breathing, moving, sensing,
    wide-eyed, cock-eared alive—
in this mysterious instant,
  at this luminous time,
    on this nurturing earth,
      this blue pearl of great price
        whirling through uncharted space,
          attended by vigilant stars;
during these days of chance and battle,
  with streaks of hope and holiness on the horizon,
    touched by nature's pleading beauty
      and friendship's steady hold.

I am so thankful to be alive—
  eyes in love with seeing,
    ears in love with hearing,
      heart in love with attending,
        mind in love with connecting;
eager to miss no message of grace
  in the ballet of beauty
    or in the cramp of struggle
      of this incredible gift of life;

attentive to all the clues of love,
daringly and outlandishly
scattered for me through Jesus's life,
overturning habit and hate;
attentive to the dreams he renews,
the wounds he heals,
the promises he nails up
for me to step out on.

I am so thankful to be alive,
thankful for those times
when the rhythms of my life
catch the cadences of your kingdom,
when there is a lightening in me
for a moment,
when the creep of courage
allows me to dare to serve the gifts
you have put in me;
thankful for the neighbors you have put beside me,
and the possibilities you have put before me;
thankful for the surge of determination to accept difficulty
not as an excuse for passivity,
but as a goad to creativity,
as the door to abundant life,
and the seed of a peace the world cannot take away,
as it takes away so much else.

I am so thankful to be alive,
O Persistent Friend, Insistent Enemy;
hold me always in the womb of mystery
and raise me again and again, forever,
to life,
and to love,
and to the claims of your kingdom.

O God of Timelessness and Time

O God of timelessness
    and time,
I thank you for my time
and for those things that are yet possible
    and precious in it:
        daybreak and beginning again,
            midnight and the touch of angels,
                the taming of demons in the dance of dreams;
a word of forgiveness,
    and sometimes a song,
for my breathing . . . my life.

Thank you
for the honesty which marks friends
    and makes laughter;
for fierce gentleness
    which dares to speak the truth in love
        and tugs me to join the long march toward peace;
for the sudden gusts of grace
    which rise unexpectedly in my wending from dawn to dawn;
for children unabashed,
    wind rippling a rain puddle,
        a mockingbird in the darkness,
            a colleague and a cup of coffee;
for all the mysteries of loving,
    of my body next to another's body;
for music and silence,
    for wrens and Orion,
        for everything that moves me to tears,
            to touching,
                to dreams,
                    to prayers;
for my longing . . . my life.

Thank you
for work
    which engages me in an internal debate
        between right and reward
    and stretches me toward responsibility
        to those who pay for my work,
    and to those who cannot pay
        because they have no work;
for justice
    which repairs the devastations of poverty;
for liberty
    which extends to the captives of violence;
for healing
    which binds up the broken bodied and broken hearted;
for bread broken
    for all the hungry of the earth;
for good news
    of love which is stronger than death;
and for peace
    for all to sit under fig trees and not be afraid;
for my calling . . . my life.

Thank you
for the sharp senses of the timeless stirring in my time,
    and your praise in my heart;
for the undeniable awareness, quick as now,
    that the need of you is the truth of me,
        and your presence with me is the truth of you,
        which sets me free
            for others,
                for joy,
                    and for you;
for your grace . . . my life . . . forever.

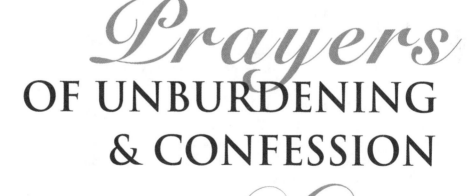

Prayers
OF UNBURDENING
& CONFESSION

Empty Me

Gracious and Holy One,
   creator of all things
      and of emptiness,
I come to you
   full of much that clutters and distracts,
      stifles and burdens me,
         and makes me a burden to others.
Empty me now
   of gnawing dissatisfactions,
      of anxious imaginings,
         of fretful preoccupations,
   of nagging prejudices,
      of old scores to settle,
         and of the arrogance of being right.
Empty me
   of the ways I unthinkingly think of myself as powerless,
      as a victim,
         as determined by sex, age, race,
            as being less than I am,
               or as other than yours.
Empty me
   of the disguises and lies
      in which I hide myself from other people
         and from my responsibility
            for my neighbors and for the world.
Hollow out in me a space
   in which I will find myself,
      find peace and a whole heart,
         a forgiving spirit and holiness,
            the springs of laughter,
      and the will to reach boldly
         for abundant life for myself
            and the whole human family.

Drive Me Deep to Face Myself

Lord, grant me your peace,
    for I have made peace
        with what does not give peace,
          and I am afraid.
Drive me deep, now,
    to face myself so I may see
that what I truly need to fear is
    my capacity to deceive
        and willingness to be deceived,
    my loving of things
        and using of people,
    my struggle for power
        and shrinking of soul,
    my addiction to comfort
        and sedation of conscience,
    my readiness to criticize
        and reluctance to create,
    my clamor for privilege
        and silence at injustice,
    my seeking for security
        and forsaking the kingdom.
Lord, grant me your peace.
Instill in me such fear of you
    as will begin to make me wise,
and such quiet courage
    as will enable me to begin to make
        hope visible,
          forgiving delightful,
        loving contagious,
          faith liberating,
        peace-making joyful
          and myself open and present
            to other people
              and your kingdom.

Loosen My Grip

O God, it is hard for me to let go,
  most times,
and the squeeze I exert
  garbles me and gnarls others.
So, loosen my grip a bit
  on the good times,
    on the moments of sunlight and star shine and joy,
that the thousand graces they scatter as they pass
  may nurture growth in me
    rather than turn to brittle memories.

Loosen my grip
  on those grudges and grievances
    I hold so closely,
that I may risk exposing myself
  to the spirit of forgiving and forgiveness
    that changes things and resurrects dreams and courage.

Loosen my grip
  on my fears
that I may be released a little into humility
  and into an acceptance of my humanity.

Loosen my grip
    on myself
that I may experience the freedom of a fool
    who knows that to believe
        is to see kingdoms, find power, sense glory;
    to reach out
        is to know myself held;
    to laugh at myself
        is to be in on the joke of your grace;
    to attend to each moment
        is to hear the faint melody of eternity;
    to dare love
        is to smell the wild flowers of heaven.

Loosen my grip
    on my ways and words,
        on my fears and fretfulness
that letting go
    into the depths of silence
        and my own uncharted longings,
I may find myself held by you
    and linked anew to all life
        in this wild and wondrous world
          you love so much,
so I may take to heart
    that you have taken me to heart.

Release Me from the Dark Fury

O Holy and Haunting Presence
whose spirit moves quietly
    but surely
in the sound and fury of the world
    and of my life,
you know me
    as rushing water knows the rock
        and releases its beauty
            to reflect new light.
Open me
    to the insistent abrasiveness of your grace,
        for I often trivialize love
            by abandoning the struggles
                which accompany its joys
            and rejecting the changes
                which lead to its fulfillments.
Release me
    from the dark fury
        of assuming I am unloved
    when the day calls for sacrifice
        and the night for courage.

Release me
    from the ominous fear
        of thinking some sin
            or failure of mine
        can separate me from you
    when life demands hard choices,
        and the battle, high risks.
Release me
    from the dangerous illusions
        of independence
    when the human family summons me
        to the realities and promises
            of interdependence
                among races, sexes, nations.
Release me
    from being possessed
        by riches I do not need
            and grievances that weary me
    when you call me to share
        my very self
            with neighbors
    and to reflect for the world
        the light of the kingdom
            within me.

What Can I Believe?

O God, I am so fragile:
    my dreams get broken,
    my relationships get broken,
    my heart gets broken,
    my body gets broken.

What can I believe,
    except that you will not despise a broken heart,
    that old and broken people shall yet dream dreams,
    and that the lame shall leap for joy,
        the blind see,
            the deaf hear.

What can I believe,
    except what Jesus taught:
    that only what is first broken, like bread,
        can be shared;
    that only what is broken
        is open to your entry;
    that old wineskins must be ripped open and replaced
        if the wine of new life is to expand.

So, I believe, Lord;
help my unbelief
    that I may have courage to keep trying
        when I am tired,
    and to keep wanting passionately
        when I am found wanting.

O God, I am so frail:
   my life spins like a top,
      bounced about by the clumsy hands
         of demands beyond my doing,
   fanned by furies
      at a pace but half a step from hysteria,
        so much to do,
           my days so few and fast-spent,
             and I mostly unable to recall
                what I am rushing after.

What can I believe,
   except that beyond the limits
      of my little prayers and careful creeds,
   I am not meant for dust and darkness,
      but for dancing life and silver starlight.

Help my unbelief
   that I may have courage
      to dare to love the enemies
         I have the integrity to make;
      to care for little else
         save my brothers and sisters of the human family;
      to take time to be truly with them,
         take time to see,
           take time to speak,
             take time to learn with them
                before time takes us;
  and to fear failure and death less
   than the faithlessness
      of not embracing love's risks.

God, I am so frantic:
    somehow I've lost my gentleness
        in a flood of ambition,
    lost my sense of wonder
        in a maze of videos and computers,
    lost my integrity
        in a shuffle of commercial disguises,
    lost my gratitude
        in a swarm of criticisms and complaints,
    lost my innocence
        in a sea of betrayals and compromises.

What can I believe,
    except that the touch of your mercy
        will ease the anguish of my memory;
    that the tug of your spirit
        will empower me to help carry now the burdens
            I have loaded on the lives of others;
    that the example of Jesus
        will inspire me to find again my humanity.

So, I believe, Lord;
help my unbelief
    that I may have courage
        to cut free from what I have been
    and gamble on what I can be,
        and on what you
            might laughingly do
                with trembling me
                    for your incredible world.

Unlock the Door of My Heart

Jesus said,
    "Your sins are forgiven;
        rise and walk."
Forgiveness is an unlocked door
    to walk through
        into a wide-whoopee-open world.
Forgiveness is a seed
    to water with new dreams and wild risks
        until it bears unexpected fruit.
Forgiveness is an enemy-friend
    to be born out of,
        a quietness beneath the clamor.
Forgiveness is a flower to smell,
    a wind at my back,
        a gull to scream with,
    a pain to laugh beneath,
        a burden that carries me.
It is I
    becoming We
        becoming Yours.
Forgiveness is a song to sing.
    O Lord,
        unlock the door of my heart.

There Are Things I Do Care About

Holy One,
most of the time
    you don't seem very close or real to me—
        only a word, an ought,
           a longing, maybe, a hope—
and, for the most part,
    I don't care much about you,
        and that is the not-so-pretty truth of it.

But there are things I do care about:
    myself mostly,
        and some people I feel close to—
           families, friends, children,
               most of all children.
I do care what happens to them.

So, I do care about love,
    about being loved,
        and about loving
           (or trying to);
and I wonder about it,
    how to do it,
        and what makes me want to do it.

With those close to me,
    I care about laughing,
        and crying,
           and learning,
               and talking honestly (a little);
        and fighting openly and fairly,
           and forgiving (a bit more),
               and admitting I want to be forgiven
                  and need to be (once in awhile).

I care about things,
    about getting them
        and being gotten by them;
And I do care about money
    and all the things I do for it,
        and with it,
            and what it does to me;
And I care about being a little freer
    of all that, somehow,
because I care about being secure
    core deep.

I care about my neighbors,
    at least some of them,
        sometimes;
and about all the things that would make it better,
    and perhaps easier
        for us to live together;
and the hard decisions and sacrifices
    it would take for that to happen.

Which means I do care about justice,
    though mostly from a distance,
        because I care about what it might require of me;
and then I get testy or silent
    but am haunted by it
because something in me
    won't let me stop caring about it,
        even though I often wish I could.

So, I care about my enemies,
    and am tired of being angry
        and suspicious so much,
            which is such a waste;
and I care about the least—
    the hungry
        and the sick
            and the terrorized
                and the exploited of the earth—
because I care about peace
    and long for it inside and out,
        and am weary of being afraid
            for myself and the children.

I care about this tiny fragile blue planet,
    this home, this mother earth and all her offspring,
        all the creatures who share the mystery of life.
And I really do care about beauty,
    about the songs in me,
        the poems, the stories;
I care deeply about
    the wondrous, puzzling,
        aching struggle
            that I am;
I care about this joy I feel
    flickering sometimes, flaring sometimes,
        when I touch hands or eyes
            or minds or sexes or souls,
                and ache, then, for more.

I care about living—
    living more fully,
        abundantly—
            and about my urgent longing for that;
I care about what makes me restless,
    makes me reach
        and stretch
            and grope for words,
                for dreams,
                    for other people,
                        and . . .
                            for you.

Holy One, you,
I do care about you,
    sometimes fiercely,
        or I wouldn't be stumbling along like this,
            trying to pray,
                trying to put myself in your way;
I care about you,
    and such is my faith,
        however faltering it is;
and I trust that, past words
    you care about all these things
        that I care about,
care about them more,
    infinitely more,
        than I care about them;
and that you care for me,
    even when I am careless
        of the things I care about.

Holy One,
there is something I wanted to tell you,
but there have been errands to run,
    bills to pay,
        arrangements to make,
            meetings to attend,
                friends to entertain,
                    washing to do . . .
and I forget what it is I wanted to say to you,
        and mostly I forget what I'm about,
            or why.
O God,
don't forget me, please,
for the sake of Jesus Christ.

Eternal One,
there is something I wanted to tell you,
but my mind races with worrying and watching,
    with weighing and planning,
        with rutted slights and pothole grievances,
            with leaky dreams and leaky plumbing
                and leaky relationships I keep trying to plug up;
and my attention is preoccupied
    with loneliness,
        with doubt,
            and with things I covet;

and I forget what it is I wanted to say to you,
    and how to say it honestly
        or how to do much of anything.
O God,
don't forget me, please,
for the sake of Jesus Christ.

Almighty One,
there is something I wanted to ask you,
but I stumble along the edge of a nameless rage,
haunted by a hundred floating fears
    of terrorists of all kinds,
        of losing my job,
            of failing,
    of getting sick and old,
        of having loved ones die,
            of dying,
    of having no one love me,
        not even myself,
    and of not being sure who I am
        or that I am worth very much,
            and . . .
I forget what the real question is that I wanted to ask,
    and I forget to listen anyway
        because you seem unreal and far away,
            and I forget what it is I have forgotten.
O God,
don't forget me, please,
for the sake of Jesus Christ.

O Father and Mother in Heaven,
perhaps you've already heard what I wanted to tell you.
What I wanted to ask is
    forgive me,
        heal me,
            increase my courage, please.
Renew in me a little of love and faith,
    and a sense of confidence,
        and a vision of what it might mean
            to live as though you were real,
                and I mattered,
                    and everyone was sister and brother.
What I wanted to ask in my blundering way is
    don't give up on me,
        don't become too sad about me,
            but laugh with me,
                and try again with me,
                    and I will with you, too.
What I wanted to ask is
    for peace enough to want and work for more,
        for joy enough to share,
    and for awareness that is keen enough
        to sense your presence
            here,
                now,
                    there,
                        then,
                            always.

I Remember Now in Silence

Lord,
plunge me deep into a sense of sadness
at the pain of my sisters and brothers
    inflicted by war,
        prejudice,
            injustice,
                indifference,
that I may learn again to cry as a child
until my tears baptize me
into a person who touches with care
those I now touch in prayer:
    victims of violence,
        of greed,
            of addictions;
    prisoners in ghettos,
        in old age,
            in sexism;
    people with broken bodies,
        with broken hearts,
            with broken lives,
whom I remember now in silence before you
because I have too often forgotten them
in the shuffle of my fretful busy-ness.

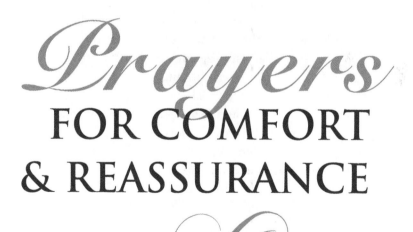

Prayers
FOR COMFORT
& REASSURANCE

Sometimes, Lord,
it just seems to be too much:
    too much violence, too much fear;
    too much of demands and problems;
    too much of broken dreams and broken lives;
    too much of war and slums and dying;
    too much of greed and squishy fatness
        and the sounds of people
            devouring each other
                and the earth;
    too much of stale routines and quarrels,
        unpaid bills and dead ends;
    too much of words lobbed in to explode
        and leaving shredded hearts and lacerated souls;
    too much of turned-away backs and yellow silence,
        red rage and the bitter taste of ashes in my mouth.
Sometimes the very air seems scorched
    by threats and rejection and decay
        until there is nothing
            but to inhale pain
                and exhale confusion.
Too much of darkness, Lord,
    too much of cruelty
        and selfishness
            and indifference . . .

Too much, Lord,
	too much,
		too bloody,
			bruising,
				brain-washing much.

Or is it too little,
	too little of compassion,
too little of courage,
	of daring,
		of persistence,
			of sacrifice;
too little of music
	and laughter
		and celebration?

O God,
make of me some nourishment
	for these starved times,
some food for my brothers and sisters
	who are hungry for gladness and hope,
that, being bread for them,
	I may also be fed
		and be full.

God . . . Are You There?

God . . . are you there?
I've been taught,
   and told I ought
      to pray.
But the doubt
   won't go away;
yet neither
   will my longing to be heard.
My soul sighs
   too deep for words.
Do you hear me?
God . . . are you there?

Are you where love is?
I don't love well,
   or often,
      anything
         or anyone.
But, when I do,
   when I take the risk,
there's a sudden awareness
   of all I've missed;
and it's good,
   it's singing good.
For a moment
   life seems as it should.
But, I forget, so busy soon,
   that it was,
      or what
         or whom.
Help me!
God . . . are you there?

How Shall I Pray?

How shall I pray?
    Are tears prayers, Lord?
    Are screams prayers,
        or groans
            or sighs
                or curses?
Can trembling hands be lifted to you,
    or clenched fists
        or the cold sweat that trickles down my back
            or the cramps that knot my stomach?
Will you accept my prayers, Lord,
    my real prayers,
        rooted in the muck and mud and rock of my life,
and not just my pretty, cut-flower, gracefully arranged
    bouquet of words?
Will you accept me, Lord,
    as I really am,
        messed up mixture of glory and grime?
Lord, help me!
Help me to trust that you do accept me as I am,
that I may be done with self-condemnation
    and self-pity,
        and accept myself.
Help me to accept you as you are, Lord:
    mysterious,
        hidden,
            strange,
                unknowable;
and yet to trust
    that your madness is wiser
        than my timid, self-seeking sanities,
and that nothing you've ever done
    has really been possible,
so I may dare to be a little mad, too.

Gather Me to Be with You

O God, gather me now
    to be with you
        as you are with me.
Soothe my tiredness;
    quiet my fretfulness;
        curb my aimlessness;
           relieve my compulsiveness;
let me be easy for a moment.

O Lord, release me
    from the fears and guilts
        which grip me so tightly;
    from the expectations and opinions
        which I so tightly grip,
that I may be open
    to receiving what you give,
        to risking something genuinely new,
           to learning something refreshingly different.

O God, gather me
    to be with you
        as you are with me.
Forgive me
    for claiming so much for myself
        that I leave no room for gratitude;
    for confusing exercises in self-importance
        with acceptance of self-worth;
    for complaining so much of my burdens
        that I become a burden;
for competing against others so insidiously
    that I stifle celebrating them
        and receiving your blessing through their gifts.

O God, gather me
    to be with you
        as you are with me.
Keep me in touch with myself,
    with my needs,
        my anxieties,
            my angers,
                my pains,
                    my corruptions,
that I may claim them as my own
rather than blame them on someone else.

O Lord, deepen my wounds
    into wisdom;
shape my weaknesses
    into compassion;
gentle my envy
    into enjoyment,
        my fear into trust,
            my guilt into honesty,
                my accusing fingers into tickling ones.

O God, gather me
    to be with you
        as you are with me.

I Want So to Belong

O God, I want so to belong;
    teach me to accept.
I want to be close;
    teach me to reach out.
I want a place where I am welcome;
    teach me to open my arms.
I want mercy;
    teach me to forgive.
I want beauty;
    teach me honesty.
I want peace;
    show me the eye of the storm.
I want truth; show me the way to question
    my unquestionable convictions.
I want joy;
    show me the way of deeper commitment.
I want life;
    show me how to die.

Sustain Me in the Coming Then

O God, empty me of angry judgments,
    and aching disappointments,
        and anxious trying,
and breathe into me
    something like quietness
        and confidence,
that the lion and the lamb in me
    may lie down together
        and be led by a trust
as straightforward as a little child.

Catch my pride and doubt off guard
that, at least for the moment,
I may sense your presence
    and your caring,
and be surprised
    by a sudden joy
        rising in me now
to sustain me in the coming then.

I Have So Few Ways to Pray

Lord,
I have so few ways to pray,
    but you have so many ways to answer.
Keep me alert
    to your unpredictable answers,
        to your unexplainable surprises,
and by your grace,
make me one of those surprises,
for the sake of the One
    who taught us the surprises
        of moving mountains,
           healing touches,
              wondrous stories,
                great banquets,
                  first suppers,
                    broken bread,
                      crosses,
                        and resurrections.

Remind Me of Your Steady Power

O God,
this is a hard time,
a season of confusion,
    a frantic rush
        to fill my closets,
           my schedule,
               and my mind,
only to find myself empty.

Give me hope, Lord,
and remind me
    of your steady power
        and gracious purposes
that I may live fully.
Renew my faith
    that the earth is not destined
        for dust and darkness,
    but for frolicking life
        and deep joy
that, being set free
    from my anxiety for the future,
I may take the risks of love
    today.

Waken in Me a Gratitude for My Life

O God, complete the work you have begun in me.
Release through me
    a flow of mercy and gentleness that will bring
    water where there is desert,
    healing where there is hurt,
    peace where there is violence,
    beauty where there is ugliness,
    justice where there is brokenness,
    beginnings where there are dead-ends.
Waken in me
    gratitude for my life,
    love for every living thing,
    joy in what is human and holy,
    praise for you.
Renew my faith that you are God
    beyond my grasp
        but within my reach;
    past my knowing
        but within my searching;
    disturber of the assured,
        assurer of the disturbed;
    destroyer of illusions,
        creator of dreams;
    source of silence and music,
        sex and solitude,
            light and darkness,
                death and life.
O Keeper of Promises, composer of grace,
grant me glee in my blood,
        prayer in my heart,
            trust at my core,
                songs for my journey,
                    and a sense of your kingdom.

I Teeter on the Brink of Endings

O God of endings,
    you promised to be with me always,
        even to the end of time.
Move with me now in these occasions of last things,
    of shivering vulnerabilities and letting go:
        letting go of parents gone,
            past gone,
                friends going,
                    old self growing;
        letting go of children grown,
            needs outgrown,
                prejudices ingrown,
                    illusions overgrown;
        letting go of swollen grudges and shrunken loves.
Be with me in my end of things,
my letting go of dead things,
    dead ways,
        dead words,
            dead self I hold so tightly,
                defend so blindly,
                    fear losing so frantically.
I teeter on the brink of endings:
    some anticipated, some resisted,
        some inevitable, some surprising,
            most painful;
    and the mystery of them quiets me to awe.
In silence, Lord, I feel now
    the curious blend of grief and gladness in me
        over the endings that the ticking and whirling of things brings;
and I listen for your leading
    to help me faithfully move on through the fear
        of my time to let go
            so the timeless may take hold of me.

Prayers
FOR RESTORATION
& RENEWAL

I Am in Need of . . . of What?

Well, God,
I made it through another sweet-sour time,
and here I am,
    nibbled,
        frazzled,
            puzzled,
                awed,
and in need of . . . of what?
    A chuckle, maybe,
        a revolution begun with a belly laugh,
            a Bronx cheer in the face of the onslaughts
                of disaster and death itself.
Such is my need;
and this is my wonder:
    Are you really as humorless,
        as grimly serious
            as I have made you out to be?
    Or do aardvarks and monkeys,
        bullfrogs and platypuses,
            puppies and porpoises,
                and people, perhaps,
    reveal the comic side of your grace,
        the playful side of your love?
Tickle me into giggling down
    the wailing walls
        of my endless grievances.
and trip up my waddling pomposities.

Lord of laughter, as of tears,
shake me awake
and teach me to laugh at myself,
    at my black-draped solemnity,
        over my petty preoccupation with success and failure,
          through all the hurt and adversity
until my laughter lures me deep
    beneath the terrors without names,
        beneath the questions without answers,
          beneath the pain without relief;
lures me deep
    to the love in me unused,
        to the strength unspent,
          to the courage untapped,
            to the dream unrisked,
              to the beauty unexpressed;
all the way down
    to the inescapable bottom,
        to the awareness that I must get on
          with being who I am
            as fully as I can,
              as unflinchingly as I can,
                as accurately as I can,
which is to say,
    as gracefully,
      as powerfully,
        as faithfully
as you have created me to be.

Make Me Simple

O Ingenious God,
I rejoice in your creation,
and pray that your Spirit touch me so deeply
that I will find a sense of self
    which makes me glad to be who I am
        and yet restless
            at being anything less
                than I can become.
Make me simple enough
    not to be confused by disappointments,
clear enough
    not to mistake busyness for freedom,
honest enough
    not to expect truth to be painless,
brave enough
    not to sing all my songs in private,
compassionate enough
    to get in trouble,
humble enough
    to admit trouble and seek help,
joyful enough
    to celebrate all of it,
        myself and others and you
through Jesus Christ our Lord.

Draw Me to Yourself

In this moment
draw me to yourself, Lord,
and make me aware
    not so much of what I've given
        as of all I have received
            and so have yet to share.
Send me forth
    in power and gladness
        and with great courage
            to live out in the world
                what I pray and profess,
that, in sharing,
    I may do justice,
        make peace,
            grow in love,
                enjoy myself,
                    other people,
                        and your world now,
                        and you forever.

Help Me Unbury Wonder

O God of the miracles,
of galaxies
and crocuses
and children,
I praise you now
from the soul of the child within me,
shy in my awe,
delighted by my foolishness,
stubborn in my wanting,
persistent in my questioning,
and bold in my asking you
to help me unbury my talents
for wonder
and humor
and gratitude,
so I may invest them eagerly
in the recurring mysteries
of spring and beginnings,
of willows that weep,
and rivers that flow
and people who grow
in such endlessly amazing
and often painful ways;
that I will be forever linked and loyal
to justice and joy,
simplicity and humanity,
Christ and his kingdom.

Let Wonder Have Its Way with Me

O God, your gracious Spirit
moves over the mysteries of living and dying
and is strangely present to me
    in the falling leaves,
        the call of the wild geese,
           a child's birth,
              the light in a friend's eyes,
                the sudden lifting of the heart,
                  and the deep longing which brings me to you now.
Make me aware of your presence
that wonder may have its way with me,
    my passion be released,
        my confidence renewed in the depths of your holiness
until, for a moment,
my longing for you be fulfilled
and I know I am really free
    to share bread and intimacy,
        to laugh and exchange mercy,
           to be at ease in my struggles,
              bold in my loving,
                brave in facing down my terror,
                  hopeful in the rising music of your kingdom,
                    joyful in my living,
                      and graceful in my life becoming
                        a song of praise ever sung to you.

O God,
let something essential happen to me,
    something more than interesting
        or entertaining,
           or thoughtful.
O God,
let something essential happen to me,
    something awesome,
        something real.
Speak to my condition, Lord,
and change me somewhere inside where it matters,
a change that will burn and tremble and heal
    and explode me into tears
        or laughter
           or love that throbs or screams
               or keeps a terrible, cleansing silence
                  and dares the dangerous deeds.
Let something happen in me
which is my real self, God.

O God,
let something essential and passionate happen in me now.
Strip me of my illusions of self-sufficiency,
    of my proud sophistications,
        of my inflated assumptions of knowledge
and leave me shivering as Adam or Eve
    before the miracle of the natural—
        the miracle of this earth
           that nurtures me as a mother
               and delights me as a lover;

the miracle of my body
  that breathes and moves,
    hungers and digests,
      sees and hears;
  that is creased and wrinkled and sexual,
    shrinks in hurt,
      and swells in pleasure;
  that works by the most amazing messages
   of what and when and how
      coded and curled in every cell
  and that dares to speak the confronting word.

O God,
let something essential and joyful happen in me now,
something like the blooming of hope and faith,
  like a grateful heart,
    like a surge of awareness
      of how precious each moment is,
that now, not next time,
now is the occasion
  to take off my shoes,
    to see every bush afire,
      to leap and whirl with neighbor,
       to gulp the air as sweet wine
until I've drunk enough
  to dare to speak the tender word:
    "Thank you";
     "I love you";
     "You're beautiful";
      "Let's live forever beginning now";
       and "I'm a fool for Christ's sake."

Gentle My Desperation

Come, Lord Jesus,
touch me
    with love, life-giving as light,
to quiet my anger a little
    and gentle my desperation,
to soften my fears some
    and soothe the knots of my cynicism,
to wipe away the tears from my eyes
    and ease the pains in my body and soul,
to reconcile me to myself
    and then to the people around me,
        and then nation to nation,
that none shall learn war any more,
    but turn to feed the hungry, house the homeless
        and care compassionately for the least of our brothers and sisters.
Reshape me in your wholeness
to be a healing person, Lord.

Come, Lord Jesus,
expand me
    by your power, life-generating as the sea,
to accept
    and use my power,
to do something I believe in
    and be something more of who I mean to be
        and can be,
to inspire me to dream and move,
    sweat and sing,
        fail and laugh,
            cuss and create,
to link my passion with courage,
    my hope with discipline,
        my love with persistence,

to enable me to learn from difficulties,
    grow in adversities,
        gain wisdom from defeats,
            perspective from disappointments,
             gracefulness from crises,
   and find joy in simply living it all fully.
Release me through your power
to be a powerful person, Lord.

Come, Lord Jesus,
startle me
    with your presence, life-sustaining as air,
to open my heart
    to praise you,
to open my mind
    to attend you,
to open my spirit
    to worship you,
to open me
    to live my life
        as authentically and boldly as you lived yours.

Come, Lord Jesus,
be with me
    in my longing;
come, stay with me
    in my needing;
come, go with me
    in my doing;
come, struggle with me
    in my searching;
come, rejoice with me
    in my loving.

Keep Me in Touch with My Dreams

O Lord,
in the turbulence
    and the loneliness
        of my living from day to day
           and night to night,
keep me in touch with my roots,
    so I will remember where I came from
        and with whom;
keep me in touch with my feelings,
    so I will be more aware of who I really am
        and what it costs;
keep me in touch with my mind
    so I will know who I am not
        and what that means;
and keep me in touch with my dreams,
    so I will grow toward where I want to go
        and for whom.

O Lord,
deliver me
    from the arrogance of assuming
        I know enough to judge others;
deliver me
    from the timidity of presuming
        I don't know enough to help others;
deliver me
    from the illusion of claiming I have changed enough
        when I have only risked little,
that, so liberated,
    I will make some of the days to come different.

O Lord,
I ask not to be delivered
    from the tensions that wind me tight,
but I do ask for a sense of direction in which to move once wound,
      a sense of humor about my disappointments,
        a sense of respect for the elegant puzzlement of being human,
          and a sense of gladness for your kingdom
            which comes in spite of my fretful pulling and tugging.

O Lord,
nurture in me
    the song of a lover,
      the vision of a poet,
        the questions of a child,
          the boldness of a prophet,
            the courage of a disciple.

O Lord,
it is said you created people
    because you love stories.
Be with me as I live out my story.

Quicken in Me a Sense of Humor

O God of gifts,
quicken in me a sense of humor
    bright enough to help me find my way
        in these tarnished times,
    fruitful enough to be made the wine of hope
        to warm the hearts of those I live with.
Make me glad to be one of a kind,
    yet one with a kind,
        called not to be more like others,
            but more of myself,
                a guerrilla of grace,
                    that, in daring to be authentic,
                        I may become more of a human-kind.

So, O God of gifts,
liberate me to share,
    without apology or arrogance,
        not only the gifts I have,
            but the gift I am.

Set Me Free

Lord of wondrous patience,
the earth has risen again,
emerging
    from a darkness
        in a way it has never quite been before;
whirling
    to a fresh time,
        an unused space;
alive
    with trembling possibilities,
        and I with it!
Such staggering grace!
Please,
nurture me in newness;
set me free from the tyrannies
    of habit
        and complaining
            and blaming;
shake from me the dusty melancholy
    of too much success and comfort,
        pride and pretense,
that, as if on the first day of creation,
I may begin to see
    the miracle of life and humanity;
to hear
    the hum of grace
        unfolding to meet all my needs,
            unexpectedly and surprisingly,
                and urging me to go on in faith
                    to whatever is next in love.

Prayers
OF COMMITMENT
& CHANGE

Pry Me Off Dead Center

O persistent God,
deliver me from assuming your mercy is gentle.
Pressure me that I may grow more human,
    not through the lessening of my struggles,
    but through an expansion of them
    that will undamn me
    and unbury my gifts.
Deepen my hurt
    until I learn to share it
    and myself
    openly,
    and my needs honestly.
Sharpen my fears
    until I name them
    and release the power I have locked in them
    and they in me.
Accentuate my confusion
    until I shed those grandiose expectations
    that divert me from the small, glad gifts
    of the now and the here and the me.
Expose my shame where it shivers,
    crouched behind the curtains of propriety,
    until I can laugh at last
    through my common frailties and failures,
    laugh my way toward becoming whole.

Deliver me
    from just going through the motions
    and wasting everything I have
    which is today,
        a chance,
            a choice,
                my creativity,
                    your call.

O persistent God,
let how much it all matters
pry me off dead center
so if I am moved inside
    to tears
        or sighs
            or screams
                or smiles
                    or dreams,
they will be real
and I will be in touch with who I am
and who you are
and who my sisters and brothers are.

Help Me to Believe in Beginnings

God of history and of my heart,
so much has happened to me during these whirlwind days:
    I've known death and birth;
    I've been brave and scared;
    I've hurt, I've helped;
    I've been honest, I've lied;
    I've destroyed, I've created;
    I've been with people, I've been lonely;
    I've been loyal, I've betrayed;
    I've decided, I've waffled;
    I've laughed and I've cried.
You know my frail heart and my frayed history —
and now another day begins.

O God, help me to believe in beginnings
and in my beginning again,
no matter how often I've failed before.

Help me to make beginnings:
    to begin going out of my weary mind into fresh dreams,
        daring to make my own bold tracks in the land of now;
    to begin forgiving
        that I may experience mercy;
    to begin questioning the unquestionable
        that I may know truth;
    to begin disciplining
        that I may create beauty;
    to begin sacrificing
        that I may accomplish justice;
    to begin risking
        that I may make peace;
    to begin loving
        that I may realize joy.

Help me to be a beginning for others,
    to be a singer to the songless,
    a storyteller to the aimless,
    a befriender of the friendless;
to become a beginning of hope for the despairing,
    of assurance for the doubting,
    of reconciliation for the divided;
to become a beginning of freedom for the oppressed,
    of comfort for the sorrowing,
    of friendship for the forgotten;
to become a beginning of beauty for the forlorn,
    of sweetness for the soured,
    of gentleness for the angry,
    of wholeness for the broken,
    of peace for the frightened and violent of the earth.

Help me to believe in beginnings,
    to make a beginning,
        to be a beginning,
so that I may not just grow old,
    but grow new
each day of this wild, amazing life
    you call me to live
        with the passion of Jesus Christ.

Breathe Restlessness into Me

Thank you for all I forget are gifts,
    not rights.
Forgive me for all the grievances
    I remember too well.
Save me from the self-pity,
    the self-seeking,
        the fat-heartedness
        which is true poverty.
Guide me, if I'm willing
    (drive me if I'm not)
        into the hard ways of sacrifice
          which are just and loving.
Make me wide-eyed for beauty,
    and for my neighbor's need and goodness;
wide-willed for peace-making,
    and for the confronting power
        with the call to compassion;
wide-hearted for love
    and for the unloved,
        who are the hardest to touch
          and need it the most.

Dull the envy in me which criticizes
    and complains life into a thousand ugly bits.
Keep me honest and tender enough to heal,
    tough enough to be healed of my hypocrisies.
Match my appetite for privilege
    with the stomach for commitment.
Teach me the great cost of paying attention
    that, naked to the dazzle of your back as you pass,
      I may know I am always on holy ground.
Breathe into me the restlessness and courage
    to make something new,
      something saving,
        and something true
that I may understand what it is to rejoice.

Teach Me Your Ways

Teach me your ways, Lord,
    that I may be open to the same Spirit
        who moved over the face of the waters
            in the first day of creation
      and moves also over the chaos of this time
        to fashion a day like this,
           a world like ours,
              a life like mine,
                a kingdom like leaven in bread,
                  like a treasure
                      buried in the fields of the daily I plow;
and make me aware of the miracles of life,
    of warm and cold,
        of starkness and order,
            of screaming wind and impenetrable silences,
                and of the unfathomable mystery of amazing grace in which I am kept.

Teach me your ways, Lord,
    that I may praise you
        for all the surprising, ingenious ways you bless me,
           and for all the wondrous gifts you give me
              through artists who introduce me to the beauty of holiness,
                who usher me into awesome worlds in which I begin to live anew
                in a fullness of pain and joy not possible before.

Teach me your ways, Lord,
    that I may accept my own talent openly,
        nurture it hopefully,
            develop it faithfully,
                and give it freely.

Teach me your ways, Lord,
    that I may love the kindness of the prophets
        and practice it toward the hungry of the world,
            the poor and sick and oppressed
    that I may learn the healing humility
        which responsibly tends the earth and all creatures therein.

Teach me your ways, Lord,
    that I may be swept up in worship with the saints,
        which surges in wonder, gratitude, and obedience,
            and shapes my life into an irrepressible YES to you,
                to all my sisters and brothers,
                    and to the presence of the kingdom among us
  until the ancient vision of mothers burns in me
        with a fire to light the world
        and warm its heart,
            through Jesus Christ,
                the singer of passionate songs,
                  the teller of powerful stories,
                  the artist of daring ways.

I Claim Your Power to Create

O Ingenious One,
it is not only creation,
    but creativity that awes me.
It is a wondrous, fearsome thing
    that you share your power to create.

O Mysterious One,
I shrink from your power,
yet I claim it;
    and it is mine by your genius
        or madness,
    this power to speak
        and have light burst upon a mind or darkness descend upon a heart;
    this power to make music
        to which souls dance or armies march;
    this power to mold and paint and carve
        and so spin out the stars by which I plot my course to heaven or to hell;
    this power to hear and touch and taste
        the love and truth by which life itself is birthed and built,
            or the hate and lies by which it shrivels and dies.

O Daring One,
it is an awesome power you've shared;
and I rejoice in the artists
    who dare to use their gift to create the beauty
        which casts this world into a more whole and holy dimension,
    who dare to breathe visions and vibrations into dullness,
        as you breathed life into dust.

O Gracious One,
it is an awesome power you've shared;
and I honor your power
    not only in pianist, poet, and painter,
        but in those whose encouragement ignites my heart,
          whose laughter lights up a room,
           whose touch fills a void,
             whose integrity inspires my will,
    whose commitment builds a church,
      whose compassion builds a community,
      whose demands stretch my soul,
        and whose love makes my day;
and I honor your power in those artists
    of kitchen and office and shop,
      of courtroom and classroom and sickroom;
in those crazy people
    who somehow know the world is always unfinished,
      and who happily risk pushing and shoving
        and tugging and pounding
        and making love to it
          until it and all of us
            come out in more glorious shape.

O Ingenious One,
it is not only creation,
    but creativity that awes me.
It is a wondrous, fearsome thing
    that you share your power to create.

Turn Your Spirit Loose

O God, turn your Spirit loose now,
    and me with it,
that I may go to where the edge is
    to face with you the shape of my mortality:
        the inescapable struggle and loneliness and pain
            which remind me
                that I am less than god after all,
                    that you have made me with hard limits,
                    limits to my strength,
                      my knowledge,
                        my days.
Facing those limits, Lord,
grant me grace
    to live to the limit
        of being unflinchingly alive,
            irrepressibly alive,
                fully alive,
        of experiencing
            every fragile,
                miraculous,
                    bloody,
                      juicy,
                        aching,
                          beautiful ounce
                          of being a human being;
of doing my duty
    and a little more;
of loving the people around me,
    my friends and my enemies;
of humbling myself to take others seriously
    and delightedly;
of applying my heart to the wisdom of simplicity,
    the freedom of honesty.

O God, turn your Spirit loose here,
    and me with it,
that I may go to where the silence is
      to face with you the utter mystery
         of questions without answers,
            pain without balm,
               sorrow without comfort,
                  and fears without relief,
                     which hound my days
                        and haunt my sleep.
Facing the mystery, Lord,
grant me grace
    to wrestle with it
      until I name the fears
        and force them to set me free
          to move on with whatever limp I'm left with;
    to wrestle with it
      until the pain teach me
        and I befriend it,
      until the silence subdues me
        into an awareness that it is holy
        and I am healed by it;
    to wrestle with it
      until I go deeper in it
        to gratitude
          for all the shapes of wholeness
            and of hope that bless me.

O God,
turn your Spirit loose now,
    and me with it,
that I may go to where the darkness is
    to face with you the terrible uncertainty of tomorrow:
        of what will happen,
            what might happen,
              what could happen,
                to me
                    and to my children
                        and to my friends,
                to my job,
                  to my relationships,
                    to my country;
      all that I cannot see, but fantasize,
        that I would prevent, but cannot,
          and so must accept as possibilities.
Facing the uncertainty, Lord,
grant me grace
    to look at it directly and openly and truly,
    to laugh at it with crazy faith
      in the crazy promise
        that nothing can separate me from your love;
    to laugh for the joy of it,
      the joy of those saving surprises
        that also stir in the darkness.
And, so, I trust,
    despite the dark uncertainty of tomorrow,
      in the light of my todays,
        in the cross,
          and in a kingdom coming,
and, so, I move on and pray on
with Jesus, my friend and redeemer.

Bring More of What I Dream

O God,
who out of nothing
    brought everything that is,
out of what I am
    bring more of what I dream
        but haven't dared;
direct my power and passion
    to creating life
        where there is death,
    to putting flesh of action
        on bare-boned intentions,
    to lighting fires
        against the midnight of indifference,
    to throwing bridges of care
        across canyons of loneliness;
so I can look on creation,
    together with you,
        and, behold,
            call it very good;
through Jesus Christ my Lord.

I Tremble on the Edge of a Maybe

O God of beginnings,
as your Spirit moved
    over the face of the deep
        on the first day of creation,
move with me now
    in my time of beginnings,
        when the air is rain-washed,
            the bloom is on the bush,
                and the world seems fresh
                    and full of possibilities,
                        and I feel ready and full.

I tremble on the edge of a maybe,
    a first time,
        a new thing,
            a tentative start,
and the wonder of it lays its finger on my lips.

In silence, Lord,
I share now my eagerness
    and my uneasiness
        about this something different
            I would be or do;
and I listen for your leading
    to help me separate the light
        from the darkness
            in the change I seek to shape
                and which is shaping me.

Go with Me in a New Exodus

O God of fire and freedom,
deliver me from my bondage
     to what can be counted
and go with me in a new exodus
     toward what counts,
but can only be measured
     in bread shared
          and swords become plowshares;
     in bodies healed
          and minds liberated;
     in songs sung
          and justice done;
     in laughter in the night
          and joy in the morning;
     in love through all seasons
          and great gladness of heart;
     in all people coming together
          and a kingdom coming in glory;
     in your name being praised
          and my becoming an alleluia,
through Jesus the Christ.

Prayers
FOR SEASONS
& HOLIDAYS

I Hold My Life Up to You Now

Patient God,
the clock struck midnight
    and I partied with a strange sadness in my heart,
        confusion in my mind.
Now, I ask you
    to gather me,
       for I realize
           the storms of time have scattered me,
             the furies of the year past have driven me,
             many sorrows have scarred me,
         many accomplishments have disappointed me,
            much activity has wearied me,
             and fear has spooked me
                into a hundred hiding places,
                  one of which is pretended gaiety.
I am sick of a string of "have-a-nice-day's."
What I want is passionate days,
    wondrous days,
       dangerous days,
         blessed days,
           surprising days.
What I want is you!

New Year's Day

Patient God,
this day teeters on the edge of waiting
    and things seem to slip away from me,
        as though everything were only memory
            and memory is capricious.
Help me not to let my life slip away from me.
O God, I hold up my life to you now,
    as much as I can,
        as high as I can,
            in this mysterious reach called prayer.
Come close, lest I wobble and fall short.
It is not days or years I seek from you,
    not infinity and enormity,
        but small things and moments and awareness,
            awareness that you are in what I am
                and in what I have been indifferent to.
It is not new time,
    but new eyes,
        new heart I seek,
            and you.

New Year's Day

Patient God,
in this teetering time,
   this time in the balance,
     this time of waiting,
make me aware of moments,
   moments of song,
     moments of bread and friends,
       moments of jokes
         (some of them on me)
           which, for a moment, deflate my pomposities;
moments of sleep and warm beds,
   moments of children laughing and parents bending,
     moments of sunsets and sparrows outspunking winter,
moments when broken things get mended
   with glue or guts or mercy or imagination;
     moments when splinters shine and rocks shrink,
     moments when I know myself blest,
       not because I am so awfully important,
         but because you are so awesomely God,
           no less of the year to come
             as of all the years past;
           no less of this moment
             than of all my moments;
           no less of those who forget you
             as of those who remember,
               as I do now,
                 in this teetering time.

O Patient God,
make something new in me,
   in this year,
   for you.

New Year's Day

Catch Me in My Scurrying

Catch me in my anxious scurrying, Lord,
and hold me in this Lenten season:
hold my feet to the fire of your grace
    and make me attentive to my mortality
        that I may begin to die now
           to those things that keep me
             from living with you
               and with my neighbors on this earth;
       to grudges and indifference,
         to certainties that smother possibilities,
          to my fascination with false securities,
            to my addiction to sweatless dreams,
              to my arrogant insistence on how it has to be;
       to my corrosive fear of dying someday
         which eats away the wonder of living this day,
          and the adventure of losing my life
           in order to find it in you.

Catch me in my aimless scurrying, Lord,
and hold me in this Lenten season:
hold my heart to the beat of your grace
    and create in me a resting place,
       a kneeling place,
         a tip-toe place

Lent

where I can recover from the dis-ease of my grandiosities
    which fill my mind and calendar with busy self-importance,
that I may become vulnerable enough
    to dare intimacy with the familiar,
        to listen cup-eared for your summons,
          and to watch squint-eyed for your crooked finger
            in the crying of a child,
              in the hunger of the street people,
                in the fear of the contagion of terrorism in all people,
              in the rage of those oppressed because of sex or race,
                in the smoldering resentments of exploited third world nations,
                in the sullen apathy of the poor and ghetto-strangled people,
              in my lonely doubt and limping ambivalence;
and somehow,
    during this season of sacrifice,
        enable me to sacrifice time
          and possessions
          and securities,
to do something . . .
    something about what I see,
        something to turn the water of my words
          into the wine of will and risk,
            into the bread of blood and blisters,
            into the blessedness of deed,
          of a cross picked up,
            a saviour followed.

Catch me in my mindless scurrying, Lord,
and hold me in this Lenten season:
hold my spirit to the beacon of your grace
    and grant me light enough to walk boldly,
        to feel passionately,
           to love aggressively;
grant me peace enough to want more,
    to work for more
        and to submit to nothing less,
          and to fear only you . . .
            only you!
Bequeath me not becalmed seas,
    slack sails and premature benedictions,
        but breathe into me a torment,
          storm enough to make within myself
          and from myself,
            something . . .
something new,
    something saving,
      something true,
a gladness of heart,
    a pitch for a song in the storm,
      a word of praise lived,
        a gratitude shared,
          a cross dared,
            a joy received.

Lent

Be with Me in My Unfolding

It is spring, Lord,
and the land is coming up green again,
   unfolding
      outside my well-drawn boundaries
         and urgent schedules.
And there is the mystery
   and the smile of it.
The willows are dripping honey color into the rivers,
and the mother birds are busy in manger nests,
and I am learning again that "for everything there is a season
   and a time for every matter under heaven."
O Lord, you have sketched the lines of spring.
Be with me in my unfolding.

It is spring, Lord,
and my blood runs warm with the song of the sap,
   longing
      for a beauty I would become.
And there is the mystery
   and the smile of it.
The buds are swelling on the bush,
   the sun is beginning to coax the color
      from where it's been curled against the cold,
        the air is sweet to the nostrils;
even the city seems to be rubbing its eyes
   from a long sleep;

and there is a promise in the season
    I know no name for
        except life.
O Lord, you have sketched the lines of spring.
Be with me in my longing.

It is spring, Lord,
and something stirs in me,
    reaching, stretching,
        groping for words,
            peeking through my defenses,
                beckoning in my laughter,
                    riding on past my fears,
                        pulsing in my music.
And there is the mystery
    and the smile of it.
Be with me in my reaching
    so I will touch or be touched,
        this time,
            by a grace, a warmth, a light,
to unfold my life to a new beginning,
    a fresh budding,
        a spring within as well as around me.
O Lord, you have sketched the lines of spring.
Be with me in my reaching.

Spring

Shock Me with Terrible Goodness

Holy One,
shock and save me with the terrible goodness of this Friday,
and drive me deep into my longing for your kingdom,
until I seek it first—
    yet not first for myself,
but for the hungry
    and the sick
        and the poor of your children,
for prisoners of conscience around the world,
for those I have wasted
    with my racism
        and sexism
            and ageism
                and nationalism
                    and religionism,
for those around this mother earth and in this city
who, this Friday, know far more of terror than of goodness;
that, in my seeking first the kingdom,
    for them as well as for myself,
        all these things may be mine as well:
things like a coat and courage
    and something like comfort,
        a few lilies in the field,
            the sight of birds soaring on the wind,
                a song in the night,
                    and gladness of heart,
the sense of your presence
    and the realization of your promise
        that nothing in life or death
            will be able to separate me or those I love,
                from your love
                    in the crucified one who is our Lord,
                      and in whose name and Spirit I pray.

Good Friday

I Praise You for This Resurrection Madness

Lord of such amazing surprises
    as put a catch in my breath
       and wings on my heart,
I praise you for this joy,
    too great for words
       but not for tears and songs and sharing;
for this mercy
    that blots out my betrayals
       and bids me begin again,
          to limp on,
             to hop-skip-and-jump on,
                to mend what is broken in and around me,
                   and to forgive the breakers;
for this YES
    to life and laughter,
       to love and lovers,
         and to my unwinding self;
for this kingdom
    unleashed in me and I in it forever,
       and no dead ends to growing,
         to choices,
           to chances,
             to calls to be just;
    no dead ends to living,
       to making peace,
         to dreaming dreams,
           to being glad of heart;
for this resurrection madness
    which is wiser than I
       and in which I see
         how great you are,
           how full of grace.
             Alleluia!

Easter

Lord,
send the gift of your Spirit
   to fill this place
      and myself
         and the world.
Touch me
   with truth
      that burns like fire,
        with beauty
           that moves me like the wind;
and set me free, Lord,
   free to try new ways of living;
      free to forgive myself and others;
        free to love and laugh and sing;
          free to lay aside my burden of security;
            free to join the battle for justice and peace;
              free to see and listen and wonder again
                at the gracious mystery of things and persons;
free to be,
   to give,
      to receive,
         to rejoice as a child of your Spirit.

And, Lord,
teach me how to dance,
   to turn around
      and come down where I want to be,
         in the arms and heart of your people
           and in you,
that I may praise and enjoy you forever.

Pentecost

Let Me Live Grace-fully

Thank you, Lord,
for this season
    of sun and slow motion,
        of games and porch sitting,
           of picnics and light green fireflies
                on heavy purple evenings;
and praise for slight breezes.
It's good, God,
as the first long days of your creation.

Let this season be for me
    a time of gathering together the pieces
        into which my busyness has broken me.
O God, enable me now
    to grow wise through reflection,
        peaceful through the song of the cricket,
           recreated through the laughter of play.

Most of all, Lord,
let me live easily and grace-fully for a spell,
    so that I may see other souls deeply,
        share in a silence unhurried,
           listen to the sound of sunlight and shadows,
                explore barefoot the land of forgotten dreams and shy hopes,
                    and find the right words to tell another who I am.

Summer

Waken in Me a Sense of Joy

O extravagant God,
in this ripening, red-tinged autumn,
waken in me a sense of joy
    in just being alive,
joy for nothing in general
    except everything in particular;
joy in sun and rain
    mating with earth to birth a harvest;
joy in soft light
    through shyly disrobing trees;
joy in the acolyte moon
    setting halos around processing clouds;
joy in the beating of a thousand wings
    mysteriously knowing which way is warm;
joy in wagging tails and kids' smiles
    and in this spunky old city;
joy in the taste of bread and wine,
    the smell of dawn,
        a touch,
            a song,
                a presence;
joy in having what I cannot live without—
    other people to hold and cry and laugh with;
joy in love,
    in you;
and that all at first and last
    is grace.

My Words Can't Carry All the Praise

Glorious God,
how curious
    and what a confession
        that we should set aside one day a year
            and call it Thanksgiving.
I smile at the presumption,
    and hope you smile, too.
But the truth is,
    Holy Friend,
        that my words can't carry all the praise
          I want them to,
            or that they should,
                no matter how many trips they make.

So this day,
    all is praise and thanks
        for all my days.
I breathe and it is your breath that fills me.
    I look and it is your light by which I see.
        I move and it is your energy moving in me.
I listen and even the stones speak of you.
    I touch and you are between finger and skin.
        I think and the thoughts are but sparks
          from the fire of your truth.
I love and the throb is your presence.
    I laugh and it is the rustle of your passing.
        I weep and your Spirit broods over me.
          I long and it is the tug of your kingdom.

Thanksgiving

I praise you, Glorious One,
for what has been, and is and will ever be:
for galaxy upon galaxy, mass and energy,
   earth and air, sun and night,
      sea and shore, mountain and valley,
         root and branch, male and female,
creature upon creature in a thousand ingenious ways,
   two-legged, hundred-legged, smooth, furry, and feathery,
      bull-frogs and platypuses, peacocks and preachers,
and the giggle of it—
   and turkeys (especially, this day, the roasted kind, not the flops)—
      and families gathered, and the thanking;
         the brave, lonely one, and the asking;
            the growling, hungry ones, and the sharing.

I praise you, Glorious One,
for this color-splashed, memory-haunted,
   hope-filled, justice-seeking,
      love-grown country
and the labors that birthed it,
   the dreams that nurtured it,
      the riches that sometimes misguide it,
         the sacrifices that await it,
            the destiny that summons it
               to become a blessing to the whole human family!

Thanksgiving

O Glorious One,
for this curious day,
 for the impulses that have designated it,
  for the gifts that grace it,
   for the gladness that accompanies it,
for my life,
 for those through whom I came to be,
  for friends through whom I hear and see
   greater worlds than otherwise I would,
for all the doors of words and music and worship
 through which I pass to larger worlds,
  and for the One who brought a kingdom to me,
I pause to praise and thank you
 with this one more trip of words
  which leaves too much uncarried,
   but not unfelt,
    unlived,
     unloved.
      Thank you!

Thanksgiving

Grant Me Your Sense of Timing

O God of all seasons and senses,
grant me your sense of timing
    to submit gracefully
        and rejoice quietly
            in the turn of the seasons.

In this season of short days and long nights,
    of gray and white and cold,
teach me the lessons of waiting:
    of the snow joining the mystery
        of the hunkered-down seeds
            growing in their sleep
                watched over by gnarled-limbed, grandparent trees
                  resting from autumn's staggering energy;
              of the silent, whirling earth
                circling to race back home to the sun.
O God, grant me your sense of timing.

In this season of short days and long nights,
    of gray and white and cold,
teach me the lessons of endings:
    children growing, friends leaving,

jobs concluding,
    stages finishing,
        grieving over,
            grudges over,
                blaming over,
                    excuses over.
O God, grant me your sense of timing.

In this season of short days and long nights,
    of gray and white and cold,
teach me the lessons of beginnings:
    that such waitings and endings
        may be a starting place,
      a planting of seeds
          which bring to birth
            what is ready to be born—
                something right and just and different,
            a new song,
              a deeper relationship,
              a fuller love—
                    in the fullness of your time.
O God, grant me your sense of timing.

Winter

I Am Silent . . . and Expectant

How silently,
how silently
the wondrous gift is given.

I would be silent now,
Lord,
and expectant. . .
    that I may receive
        the gift I need,
           so I may become
                the gifts others need.

Advent

Let the Star of Morning Rise

Lord God,
in the deepest night
there rises the star of morning,
    of birth,
        the herald of a new day you are making,
a day of great joy dawning
    in yet faint shafts
        of light and love.

I hear whispers of peace in the stillness,
fresh breezes of promise
    stirring,
winter sparrows
    chirping of life,
a baby's cry
    of need
        and hope—
            Christmas!

In the darkness I see the light
    and find in it comfort,
        confidence,
            cause for celebration,
for the darkness cannot overcome it;
and I rejoice to nourish it
    in myself,
        in other people,
            in the world
for the sake of him
    in whom it was born
        and shines forever,
            even Jesus the Christ.

Christmas

Title Index

About the Author

The Rev. Dr. Theodore W. Loder was the senior minister of one of Philadelphia's most unusual churches, the First United Methodist Church of Germantown (FUMCOG), for almost thirty-eight years. With imagination and intensity, Loder led FUMCOG to the fore-front of artistic endeavors, political activism, and social justice. His congregation has been a Public Sanctuary Church, a founding church of the Covenant Against Apartheid in South Africa, a Reconciling Congregation that advocates for the rights of homosexual persons.

Loder's own social action grows out of a long history of involvement in social causes, including marching with Dr. Martin Luther King Jr. in the sixties. Loder is cofounder of Metropolitan Career Center (a job-training program for high school dropouts); cofounder of Plowshares (a non-profit housing renovation corporation); and cofounder of Urban Resource Development Corporation (an ecumenical effort to rehabilitate abandoned houses). He has also served on the Philadelphia Mayor's Advisory Commission of Children and Families.

For many people who have "given up" on the church, Loder brings a breath of fresh air. His blend of scholarship (cum laude degree from Yale Divinity School, a university fellow of the Yale Graduate School, and two honorary doctorates) and creativity (named by the National Observer as "One of America's Outstanding Creative Preachers") stimulate his refreshing openness to hard questions, to change, to relevance, to justice, and to joy. Dr. Loder currently serves on the National Advisory Board of the National Council of the Churches of Christ in the U.S.A.

About the Artist

An internationally known painter, Ed Kerns is professor of Art and Chair of the Department at Lafayette College in Easton, Pennsylvania. He has mounted more than thirty one-person shows in galleries in New York, Philadelphia, and other major cities. He has also participated in more than 150 group exhibitions in the United States, France, Italy, Switzerland, and Mexico. His work is in numerous public and corporate collections and has been reviewed in many journals, magazines, and newspapers. Kerns, whose interests include painting and digital imagery, was awarded the Clapp Professorship in 1988. Through scholar research projects, independent studies, and honors projects, he has mentored more than four hundred students.

If you've enjoyed Ted Loder's prayers in Guerrillas of Grace, here's a sampling of prayers from his other books.

Excerpt from *My Heart in My Mouth: Prayers for Our Lives*

We Dare to Ask

We ask only a few things more, O God,
    a few small, mustard-seed size, faithful, saving things:
        to walk with you in each moment
            without plotting for tomorrow,
                and so to really consider the birds of the air,
                  the lilies of the field,
                    and find the treasures hidden
                      in the round of the daily;
to learn by leaning into your Spirit
    to be present to others without preoccupation,
        to engage without having to win,
            to disagree without being judgmental,
to accept outcomes without despair
    to succeed or fail without misplacing hope,
        to tune to the bracing hum of the stars,
to fathom enough
    without dismissing fathomless mystery
        of your creation, our brothers and sisters,
            and the grace and mercy and power
                of your embrace that holds close,
                  each small one of us,
                    and everything all together;
                  in Jesus's name,
                    Amen.

Excerpt from *Wrestling the Light: Ache and Awe in the Human Divine Struggle*

Crazed into Holy Awareness

Come, Lord Jesus,
    confront me as a prophet:
        disturb my indifference,
            expose my practiced phoniness,
                shatter my brittle certainties,
                    deflate my arrogant sophistries
and craze me into a holy awareness
    of my common humanity
        and so of my bony, bloody need
            to love mercy,
              do justly,
                and walk humbly with you
                  —and with myself,
trusting that whatever things it may be too late for,
    prayer is not one of them,
        nor a chance,
            nor change,
                nor passion,
                    nor laughter,
nor starting yet again
    to risk a way to be together,
nor a wild, far-sighted claim
    that this human stuff of yours
        is stronger still than fail or time,
        graced to share a kingdom
            and spirited for you.